FEEL THE FORCE

Ride that ROLLERCOASTER!

Forces at an Amusement Park

Richard and Louise Spilsbury

raintree
a Capstone company — publishers for children

Raintree is an imprint of Capstone Global Library Limited, a company incorporated in England and Wales having its registered office at 7 Pilgrim Street, London, EC4V 6LB – Registered company number: 6695582

www.raintree.co.uk
myorders@raintree.co.uk

Edited by Helen Cox Cannons and Holly Beaumont
Designed by Philippa Jenkins
Original illustrations © Capstone Global Libary Ltd 2015
Illustrated by HL Studios, Witney, Oxon
Picture research by Tracy Cummins
Production by Helen McCreath
Originated by Capstone Global Library Ltd
Printed and Bound in China by Leo Paper Group

ISBN 978 1 406 29647 1
19 18 17 16 15
10 9 8 7 6 5 4 3 2 1

British Library Cataloguing in Publication Data
A full catalogue record for this book is available from the British Library.

Acknowledgements
We would like to thank the following for permission to reproduce photographs: Alamy Images: Gaertner, 31, imageBROKER, 14, Kim Karpeles, 37, Stockshoot, 40; AP Photo: HO, 19, Wong Maye-E, 39; Capstone Press: HL Studios, 7, 15, 23, 27, Karon Dubke, 10, 11, 24, 25, 32, 33; Corbis: Macduff Everton, 12, 42 Middle, REUTERS/Dave Kaup, 13; Dreamstime: Gow927, 29; Getty Images: ATABOY, 6, 43 Bottom, Johannes Simon, 17, Zia Soleil, 36; Rex USA: Mikael Buck/Rex, 38; Courtesy of Simworx Limited: www.siwmorx.co.uk, 34; Shutterstock: 2009fotofriends, 8, 42 Top, jabiru, Front Cover, Racheal Grazias, 4, 21, Ruslan Kerimov, 18, Ta Khum, 9; SuperStock: imageBROKER, 30; Thinkstock: Jupiterimages, Design Element, 42 Bottom, Marcio Silva, 26, 43 Top, Design Element, Purestock, 5; Wikimedia: flickr/themeparkgc, 41.

We would like to thank Patrick O'Mahony for his invaluable help in the preparation of this book.

Every effort has been made to contact copyright holders of material reproduced in this book. Any omissions will be rectified in subsequent printings if notice is given to the publisher.

Contents

Some words are shown in bold, **like this**. You can find out what they mean by looking in the glossary.

What is the lure of the park?

Where can you plummet to the ground, hang upside down, spin around, bump and get splashed, all in one day? No, not in a waterfall or an enormous washing machine, but at an amusement park! Millions of people visit amusement parks each year to experience a variety of thrills all in one place. Never mind the queues, some of these could be the rides of your life.

Motion and forces

The one thing all the rides at an amusement park have in common is motion. Things only move with a push or pull. Without these **forces**, objects stay still or they keep on moving just as they were. All forces result from the interactions between two objects. Most forces involve contact – you kick a stationary football and it rolls or flies away.

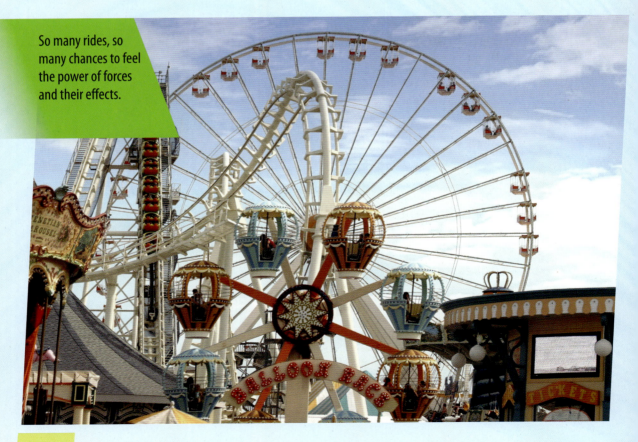

So many rides, so many chances to feel the power of forces and their effects.

Experiencing the forces of the amusement park feels dangerous, but it is safe fun.

Forces work in pairs. When the forces acting on an object are equal, or **balanced**, then the object stays in the same place or moves at a constant speed. To make an object start moving, or to change its speed or direction, we have to make one force larger than another so they are **unbalanced**. Half the fun of the rides at an amusement park is the way they speed us up and slow us down, lift us high and drop us suddenly. So exactly what forces are at work?

SPEED AND ACCELERATION

Speed is a measure of how fast something is going. Kick off on a skateboard and it would keep going at that speed forever — if there weren't other forces to slow it down. These include the force caused by its wheels rubbing against the ground, called **friction**. But if you kept pushing while the skateboard was moving, it would get faster. The rate of change of speed is called **acceleration**.

Can you feel the force?

The big cheese amongst the forces in action at an amusement park is also the one that keeps us on Earth: **gravity**. Wherever you are and whatever you're up to on Earth, gravity is pulling you towards the ground. Gravity is a **non-contact force**. We cannot feel it directly, but we do feel it indirectly. Sit on a chair and you can feel the upwards push of the wood, steel or plastic that the chair is made from resulting from the downwards pull on your body. That's what we feel as weight.

On a downwards rollercoaster ride, you feel the pull of gravity towards Earth as the push of the safety bar into your stomach or chest.

TERMINAL VELOCITY

When skydivers jump from a plane, they speed up as they fall. They reach a top speed of around 240 kilometres (150 miles) per hour just 12 seconds after jumping. We call this speed **terminal velocity**. They reach terminal velocity when their weight is balanced by air resistance.

Seconds falling	Metres per second of falling
1	10
2	20
3	30
4	40

gravity

air resistance

A bungee jumper comes to a brief stop in mid-air when the upwards pull of the elastic cord equals gravity. When these forces are unbalanced they fly upwards again!

Falling objects

We can use gravity to move. When you drop from the top point of a rollercoaster or a swingboat ride, gravity pulls you and the seat you're in downwards. The force of gravity also causes things to speed up as they fall, which is what helps to make rides so exciting – and scary! This is because the force of gravity causes acceleration when a moving object goes downhill.

The reason things don't just keep falling faster and faster when they are dropping downwards is that the opposing forces act to slow them down. These include the upwards push of air, or **air resistance**. A rollercoaster track also has brakes to slow down its movement for safety, but you will still feel the fear!

Why do I feel lighter as I fall?

Screams ring in your ears as you fall and you feel strangely light as the ground hurtles towards you. These are the unforgettable sensations of a trip on a freefall ride or drop tower. On a freefall ride:

- passengers are safely strapped in seats in a gondola or car
- powerful motors pull the car up a **vertical** track up to 126 metres (415 feet) above the ground
- the car stops, leaving passengers hanging in mid-air
- brakes are released and the car falls.

At zero G, people feel lighter even though they are the same **mass**. This is because there is less upward force acting to slow them down than if they were on the ground.

VOMIT COMET!

Astronauts experience zero G (zero gravity) in space because the pull of gravity from Earth is much weaker. They train for spending time in space in special aeroplanes that fly very high and then dive downwards. Inside the aeroplane, people can float around and experience weightlessness for several minutes in zero-G conditions before the plane has to level out. People who are not used to the feeling often feel sick and even vomit. That's how the plane got its name!

G-force

G-force is a way of describing the forces acting on someone in comparison to gravity. In the first few seconds of falling, people in a gondola or car feel as if their seats are dropping away. They experience **weightlessness** because they and their seats are accelerating at the same rate. They feel no upwards push from the seat and experience **zero G** even though gravity is still pulling them to Earth.

Slowing down

Cars don't crash into the ground on a freefall ride because tracks gradually curve towards the ground. The upwards push from the track slows the car's acceleration. Then it reaches a horizontal stretch of track and the brakes go on to **decelerate** the car until it reaches a standstill.

ACTIVITY: Weightless water

Try this simple demonstration of zero G using a cup of water. It is best to do it with two people and in a place where it is all right to spill water, such as outside or over a large bucket.

1 Make a hole about ½ cm (¼ in.) in diameter half-way down the cup using the hole punch or pencil. (Sharp pencils can also pierce skin, so ask an adult for help to avoid any injuries.)

ADULT HELP

2 One person operates the video camera and the other holds the cup.

3 Cover the hole with a finger, fill the cup with water and record what happens when you uncover the hole.

4 Climb CAREFULLY on the chair and repeat step 3, but drop the cup as you uncover the hole.

5 The fall only lasts a few seconds, so you may have to repeat until you get some good film of what happens. Repeat step 1 if your cup breaks when hitting the ground.

Conclusion

It is easier to see what happens if you watch the recordings in slow motion. Gravity pulls on water in the cup, but it only spills out when the hole is uncovered. This is because there is no balancing force pushing back on the water. Once the water level is below the hole, it stops pouring out. Water does not come out of the open hole while the cup falls. This is because the water is accelerating as fast as the cup, and the downwards force of gravity is balanced by the upwards push from the cup. The water shoots out once the cup hits the ground because it topples over.

How do I slide so fast?

For gentler sliding fun, you can take a ride on the helter-skelter. But for maximum speed – and a soaking – always choose the water slide.

Working against gravity

A slide is a slope that applies a force working against gravity. On a shallow slide, the downwards pull of gravity is only just bigger than the upwards push from the slide, so you slip down slowly. On a steep slide, there is very little upwards push from the slide, so you slide down quickly. All water slides have sides so you don't slip off the edges as you move along them.

SLOWING DOWN WITH FRICTION

The brakes that control and stop many amusement park rides work using friction. Powerful electric machines push pads against metal underneath the moving cars or gondolas to increase contact. Designers may also use water to increase friction. After a steep water slide, riders sometimes enter a water-filled canal to slow them down.

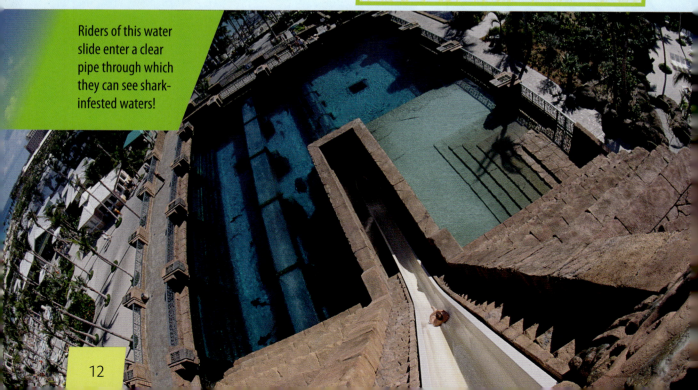

Riders of this water slide enter a clear pipe through which they can see shark-infested waters!

Making contact

A book slides faster across a polished hard floor than a carpet because of the contact force called friction. Friction acts in the opposite direction to motion. It is greater when sliding faster and when one or both of the surfaces are rough as there is greater contact between them. Friction burns can happen on playground slides because motion energy is converted to heat energy due to friction. Imagine this happening on a steep slide tens of metres long!

Reducing the rub

Slide designers reduce friction and increase speed at amusement parks in different ways. On a helter-skelter, people slide on smooth mats that protect them from any friction burns. Water slides have a constant flow of water trickling down the slide. This prevents friction by forming a slippery water layer between rider and slide.

On some enormous water slides, passengers shoot down in rafts for added protection from any bumps.

13

Am I going to fly off this ride?

Some amusement park rides put you in a spin. Scramblers and octopuses move very fast in circles and riders feel like they are going to fly off the ride. There is one thing clearly to blame: **centripetal force**.

What is centripetal force?

This is a force that comes into play when acceleration happens in a curve or a circle. Centripetal force pushes moving objects inwards towards the centre of the curve. Imagine you are sitting on a spinning scrambler. As you spin in one direction, you are actually moving outwards at right angles to the path of the curve at any point. You don't fly off because of centripetal force pulling you inwards along the arm of the scrambler.

Try as you might, it is difficult to escape the feeling of being thrown out of the car until the scrambler slows down and the centripetal force gets smaller.

USING CENTRIPETAL FORCE

Amusement parks are not the only places where centripetal force is in demand. It is often used to separate materials because the force is greater on objects with greater density, or mass, for a given size. For example, centripetal force separates the water from the clothing in a spin drier.

Centripetal force

Direction of movement of passenger on scrambler without centripetal force to pull them towards the centre

As passengers move on circular paths on the scrambler, they experience the effects of varying centripetal forces through both the small and large arms.

Circular path of small arm

Circular path of large arm

The centripetal experience

You experience the centripetal force as a strong push in your side from the edge of the car as you travel around a bend or roundabout. Centripetal force is greater when an object is moving faster and also when the distance from the centre of rotation to the object is smaller. Ride designers make passengers feel changing centripetal force by having small rotating arms on larger rotating arms. They also increase the sense of danger by making passengers in one car spin very close to those in others.

Why is the ground opening up?

You start a ride on the rotor, vortex or gravitron by walking inside a circular room and standing against the wall. Once several riders are inside, the door shuts and it gradually spins faster and faster. After awhile, the floor of the room opens up, yet you do not slip down the wall. You feel pinned there. What's going on?

Speed to stick

Riders stick to the wall owing to centripetal force and friction. The rotor spins at over 20 complete **revolutions** per minute. At this speed, there is strong centripetal force. This increases the contact of their bodies against the rotor wall so much that the forces are balanced. This means the riders won't fall or slide down the wall once the floor opens. Sliding down happens gradually once the ride slows down and gravity gets the upper hand!

Evolution of the rotor

The rotor was invented in 1949, but it was not the first popular spinning amusement park ride. The joy wheel from the early 20th century, for example, was a conical, polished disc riders sat on that spun around faster and faster. It gradually threw all the riders off into the crowd because the ride had no walls!

WHAT IS CENTRIFUGAL FORCE?

The outwards pull we feel on the rotor, scrambler or any ride that happens in a circle is often called centrifugal force. But most scientists agree that this force does not exist. They say that you or any object can only move in a circle if there is an inward centripetal force stopping you flying off in a straight line. What you feel is simply your body's interpretation of that inwards push.

The rotor ride is a popular feature of the German Oktoberfest celebrations. You can ride upright on the rotor, at an angle or even upside down!

How does a rollercoaster work?

Most people go to amusement parks for the rollercoaster. What other ride gives you high speeds, zero-g straight falls, extreme turns and twists, hanging upside-down and other sensations all in one package?

Building a ride

Vehicles called cars move along tracks supported by giant beams, columns or other strong structures. The tracks and supports can be made largely of wood, but most are usually all steel. Cars have seats for riders that can be mounted on top or hang underneath. Some even spin around during the ride. The cars roll along the track on tough plastic wheels that produce low friction, which helps them move fast. There are wheels on the top, side and bottom of the track so that they grip the car to the track whichever way it is thrown during the ride.

Getting started

Once the riders are all safely buckled in, most rollercoaster cars are pulled upwards to the top of the first hill. Most rollercoasters have a loop of tough chain moved around wheels turned by electric motors. The chain is continually moving up the hill. Metal hooks underneath each car attach it to the chain to hitch a ride to the top. Some rollercoasters have launch systems using magnets, the push of compressed air or other forces to speed them up the hill.

Rollercoaster cars have wheels above and below to make sure the train grips to the tracks even when taking tight corners or hanging upside down.

18

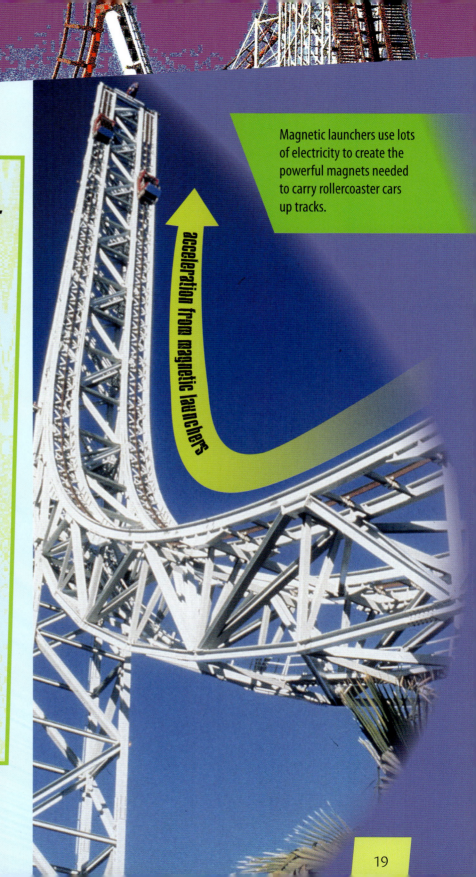

MAGNET BLAST-OFF

The fastest catapult launch rollercoasters can accelerate from 0–240 kilometres (0–150 miles) per hour in just 5 seconds. They have special electric motors to create powerful magnets underneath the car and on the track below. By changing the electricity flow, the magnets pull towards or push away from each other. The cars can speed along the tracks using these pushes and pulls.

acceleration from magnetic launchers

Magnetic launchers use lots of electricity to create the powerful magnets needed to carry rollercoaster cars up tracks.

What happens during the first fall?

At the top of the first big hill, the rollercoaster cars are standing alone. There is no more power from motors to move them along until the end of the ride. But how does a heavy rollercoaster get the energy it needs to keep going?

Storing and using energy

You might not know it, but a rollercoaster rising up a hill is busy storing energy. Energy is the ability to do work. The stored energy in the rollercoaster is **potential energy**, which results from its height above the ground. It has more if it goes higher because gravity will have a greater distance to use the energy to speed the rollercoaster downhill. The potential energy then changes into movement, or **kinetic energy**. A rollercoaster has its biggest store of this as it speeds into the foot of the first hill.

Rising again

Then rollercoaster cars often rise up another hill. This is when most of the kinetic energy starts to change back into potential energy. The upwards movement is slowed not only by the downwards pull of gravity but also by the slight friction between the wheels and the track, and air resistance. But people design rollercoasters so that the height of the first hill allows cars to store enough energy to not come to a halt until the end of the ride.

CONSERVATION OF ENERGY

Turn on a switch and electrical energy turns to light energy from a lamp. A car engine changes chemical energy in fuel into kinetic energy. Energy never disappears — it just changes form. We call this conservation of energy. In any machine, not all energy changes into the form that is needed. For example, laptop computers give off heat energy as they use electrical energy for computing tasks.

decreasing potential energy

increasing kinetic energy

A rollercoaster is an energy-converting scream machine!

friction and air resistance

gravity

What happens in a loop-the-loop?

Climb steeply, travel backwards upside-down, and then plummet downhill. This is what happens in a loop-the-loop. What is amazing about this rollercoaster feature is that it packs a punch by changing forces in a trip lasting just a few seconds.

On a loop-the-loop, one second you're feeling heavier than ever and the next as light as a feather. This is because of acceleration due to gravity and centripetal forces.

centripetal force

acceleration force

gravity

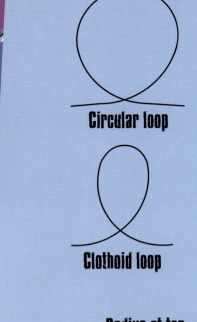
SAFETY CURVE

In the past, rollercoaster designers made completely circular loops, but they found that riders experienced unpleasantly high G-forces because of the high inwards acceleration needed to complete the feature. Today's rollercoasters have teardrop-shaped curves, called clothoid loops, which are safer and more fun to ride.

The G-force journey

On entering the loop, the car's acceleration force is pointing forwards and gravity is pointing downwards. The upwards push from the seat makes you feel heavier than ever. You are experiencing high G-forces. In an instant, the car is pointing upwards and gravity is pulling downwards. Centripetal acceleration is making you feel as if you are being pushed against the side of the loop. Then you are hanging upside down and briefly experience near zero G because there is no upwards force to push against gravity. The G-force then rises as the car zooms downwards and reaches the end of the loop-the-loop.

The energy flip

The loop-the-loop is not only a place where forces change, but also where energy changes form from kinetic to potential in an instant. But it can only work if the rollercoaster car accelerates fast and has plenty of kinetic energy to carry it upside down through the top of the loop. Without the right speeds, cars would slow and not complete the ride.

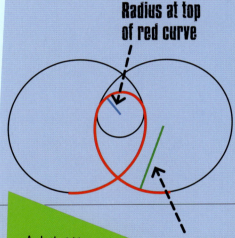

Radius at top of red curve

Radius at bottom of red curve

A clothoid loop has a smaller radius at the top, forming a tighter curve. This makes the car accelerate faster when it is upside down. The shallower curves at the sides slow the car slightly so it does not lose control going in or out of the loop-the-loop.

ACTIVITY: Loop-the-bucket

Rollercoaster designers say that people would not fall out of rollercoaster cars upside-down at the top of a loop-the-loop if they had no safety bars, owing to the forces holding them in their seats. It's not advisable to test this out, but you can carry out a simple experiment to demonstrate the forces in action.

> **You will need:**
> - a small plastic bucket with a handle
> - about 1 m (3 ft.) of thick, sturdy string
> - 20 pennies

1 Tie the string with a secure knot to the centre of the bucket handle. Adjust the string length so that you can hold one end with the bucket around 10 cm (4 in.) above the ground.

2 Put one penny in the bucket. Stand in enough space so you can swing the bucket safely. Swing the bucket forward, then backwards with bigger and bigger swings. When the bucket is swinging high, start to rotate the bucket vertically in one direction in complete loop-the-loops.

!

SAFETY! Make sure there is no one else around when you start swinging the bucket!

3 Observe what happens to the penny. What happens when you swing the bucket more slowly? Finish the demonstration with gradually smaller swings before bringing the bucket to rest.

4 Now, repeat steps 2 and 3 using 20 pennies in the bucket. What was different this time?

Conclusion

The bucket travels in a circle because of centripetal force through the string towards your hand and shoulder. Objects stay inside the bucket owing to the pull from its base towards them, opposing centripetal force. Pennies stay inside even when the bucket is upside down because the centripetal force is greater than the pull of gravity on its contents. You should find that you need to pull harder on the string and spin the bucket faster to make more pennies, with a greater total mass, stay inside the bucket. When the speed of rotation is too low, the string goes slack and the bucket cannot complete loops. Then the coins could tumble out.

What rollercoaster features are there?

Without features like hills and loop-the-loops, a trip on a rollercoaster would be no more exciting than a train ride. Rollercoaster designers have invented all sorts of features to surprise and excite riders on their visits to the amusement park.

What is a corkscrew?

A corkscrew is a series of twisty downhill turns. Looking down the track, they look like lots of concentric circles and from the side like a spring that has been stretched out. In a sequence, they make riders confused about which way up they are and let them experience lots of G-forces. Unlike loop-the-loops, riding a corkscrew maintains kinetic energy for the rest of the ride.

You can see three coils of the large corkscrew in this rollercoaster ride. Just imagine how it would feel flying through them!

Batwing

Pretzel loop
or knot

Immelmann loop or
sidewinder

Cobra roll

Upside-down features

Sea serpent, pretzel roll, inverted top hat, flying snake dive and batwing. Designers have created lots of loops, dives, twists and roll features with unusual names that are often based on their shapes. These features are called **inversions** because they are included on rides to flip riders upside-down. One of the most famous inversions is called the Immelmann loop, which is named after a World War I fighter pilot's flying manoeuvre. Like many inversions, it works by making the track twist from the top of its supports to the underside. This makes the car roll over as it moves along.

Special effects

The thrill of the rollercoaster also relies on special effects. Some rollercoasters go inside buildings or tunnels where it is dark. Other rollercoasters travel through water-filled splashdowns. Some cars have scoops that make water shoot upwards in jets when they pass through the water. But one of the most dramatic special effects is much simpler. A headchopper is a piece of track or support that the rollercoaster runs under. Most riders duck, but they easily fit through the gap under a headchopper without losing their heads!

How do bumper cars work?

Bumper cars, or dodgems, are plastic cars with small wheels that are hidden by a thick rubber bumper all the way around. When you press the floor pedal or accelerator, the car moves across the racetrack using an electric motor. If bumper cars used electrical energy through cables to power their motors, the cables would get tangled up. Batteries would be heavy and keep running down. So bumper cars get the energy from around them. In some dodgem rides the pole on the car touches the metal mesh ceiling and brushes under the car to touch the floor. This completes an **electrical circuit** so that electricity can flow into the motor. In other dodgem rides, the circuit is completed through brushes on the car and metal bars built into the floor. The steering wheel can be turned all the way around to go forwards, sideways and in reverse.

Dodgem forces

Bumper cars at rest have balanced forces. Pressing the accelerator unbalances the forces, as motion in one direction is greater than the force of friction from the wheels on the track in the other direction. When another car crashes into it, the forces in both cars become further unbalanced. They may move faster, slow down or change direction after the impact.

GRAPHITE

Graphite is a material made from carbon. In graphite, the carbon particles are arranged in sheets that are weakly linked to each other. That means they can slide over each other easily. Pencil leads are made from graphite because the layers can easily rub off on to paper. Many dodgem tracks are sprinkled with graphite powder as this helps to reduce friction under the car wheels.

You can feel the force when bumper cars collide and bounce off each other!

bounce (reaction)

bounce (reaction)

Rubber bumper

thrust (action)

thrust (action)

How does motion change after a bump?

When bumper cars collide, you can feel your head or your whole body snapping towards the other car. The jolt happens because, even though the car has stopped, the mass of your body is continuing in the previous direction of motion. This resistance to a change in direction is called **inertia**.

Inertia is greater in heavier objects, like people. So when a heavy rider in one car bumps a lighter rider's car, the lighter rider will jolt more. Their car is also pushed away more than the heavy one because it requires less force to do so. When cars are of equal weight, they will bounce off each other by an equal distance.

The jolt of a dodgem impact rarely hurts and riders aren't thrown out of the car because they are wearing seatbelts.

NEWTON'S LAWS AND DODGEMS

Sir Isaac Newton was a scientist. In the 17th century, he wrote three laws that describe all motion in action, including those on a dodgem ride.

	What the law says	What it does on the dodgems
FIRST LAW	Every moving or resting object continues moving or resting unless an outside force acts on it.	You feel a jolt when bumper cars collide.
SECOND LAW	The greater the mass of an object the harder it is to change its speed.	Lighter people are jolted and shunted more than heavier ones on dodgems.
THIRD LAW	For every action, there is an equal and opposite reaction.	When one bumper car hits another, they both move in opposite directions.

Soak up the shock

The rubber bumpers around the cars are not there for decoration. Their job is to absorb some of the impact. Seatbelts also prevent inertia making occupants fly out or bang into things. The bumper also has another trick up its sleeve. It changes an intense short bump into a longer-lasting experience.

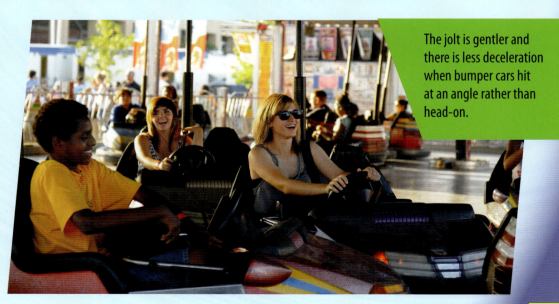

The jolt is gentler and there is less deceleration when bumper cars hit at an angle rather than head-on.

ACTIVITY: Floating dodgems

Construct a very basic bumper car that uses a layer of air to push it up and reduce the force of friction underneath.

1 Push the CD on a smooth surface, such as a table, floor or kitchen surface. How far did it go?

2 Ask for an adult's help and stick the sports bottle lid over the hole in the CD using the hot glue gun. The idea is to create an airtight seal between the CD and the bottle lid.

3 Push down the top of the bottle lid to close it. Now inflate the balloon, twist the end to stop air escaping and stretch it over the lid.

4 Place the modified CD on the smooth surface, pull up the lid to release air from the balloon and push the CD with the same force as before. Did it move more smoothly and faster than the CD with no balloon?

5 Repeat the demonstration using the larger balloon, and then increase the car's mass using some plasticine on top of the CD. How did its movement change?

Conclusion

The airflow from the balloon creates a cushion of moving air between the underside of the disc and the surface underneath. This lifts the CD and reduces contact between the materials. With less friction, the balloon dodgem can move faster and with less effort. As the balloon empties, the rubber is less stretched and pushes less on the remaining air inside, so friction increases. With a larger balloon, the air cushion should last longer. With extra weight on the CD, the airflow from the balloon should be too weak to lift its greater mass.

How does a simulator ride work?

Riders on one of the most popular amusement park machines get their thrills without actually going anywhere. A **simulator** ride uses a combination of moving seats and onscreen action to trick the riders' senses into believing they are experiencing extreme forces.

Riders on a simulator sit in the dark apart from the onscreen action. The movements of the simulator trick them into thinking they are having a real ride.

Moving box

The simulators at most amusement parks are enclosed boxes, sometimes shaped like spacecraft. Inside there are rows of seats for riders that face a screen. Underneath there are several powerful **hydraulic jacks** supporting the simulator. Liquid is forced at high pressure inside these jacks to push the end up or down. By mounting the jacks at different points on the simulator, it can be tilted in any direction.

Ride in the dark

The movements of the simulator are coordinated with what happens during a video presentation on the screen. Riders sit in the dark and view a journey on a train, plane, spaceship or other vehicle. It can be a film of a real ride but it is often a realistic 3D animation. Riders view the movement as if they are looking forward from the front of the vehicle. The jacks tip the simulator backwards and forwards so riders feel the journey as changing forces from their seats.

PILOT TRAINERS

The first simulators were built for pilots to learn about flying without the expense and danger of actually being in the air. Early 20th century simulators were model planes with **cockpits**, in which trainee pilots could operate levers to make the plane move up and down. By the 1980s, pilots could simulate flying in realistic cockpits, using controls that moved miniature cameras over highly detailed models of landscapes. Today's simulators are like sophisticated versions of amusement park rides, in which the trainees are controlling realistic action in 3D on wrap-around screens and feeling forces from movements of the simulator.

Experiencing a ride

How we feel the rides at an amusement park depends on many senses working together. Much of this is visual. Light **receptors** in our eyes detect changing patterns of light and colour that our brains use to interpret the world around us. Our ears also hear changing volumes of noises to work out where we are.

Feeling the forces

We can also feel forces because of what goes on inside our **inner ears**. When our heads move, fluid shifts through narrow canals in our ears and bends tiny hairs that contain movement receptors. Even if our eyes are closed, our brains interpret these movements to detect rotation. Other pressure receptors around our bodies, such as those in skin, muscles and joints, help us feel pushes and pulls caused by changes in motion.

Simulator trickery

A simulator tricks these senses. Inside, the only sights and sounds are from the screen, so riders get no clues about their real position from the real world. But making the images of the virtual onscreen surroundings fly past, and tilting the seats backwards to increase the push on their backs, makes riders feel they are accelerating forwards. Simulators can also fool you into thinking you are turning sharply, diving and decelerating. However, they cannot fool riders' inner ears that they are rotating, however realistic the movement appears onscreen!

Some people feel sick on amusement park rides such as the pendulum because their senses are confused!

MOTION SICKNESS

On a pendulum or gondola ride, you see a regular motion and remain the same distance from other riders. Yet your inner ears and pressure receptors, including those in the stomach, detect acceleration and frequent changes in G-forces. So your brain gets confused and it sends stress chemicals to the stomach. That's why you might feel motion sickness!

Can I have thrills without spills?

The fear you feel on the most extreme rides is your body's natural response to its sense of danger. But don't worry. Amusement parks focus on safety as well as fun.

Park workers regularly inspect the condition of tracks and maintain the wheels, brakes, motors and other moving parts on rides.

Before being used in ride construction, materials are carefully tested for their strength and durability.

Safety in numbers

Amusement parks are very popular. In the US alone, around a third of a billion people visit amusement parks each year. Of these, only around 1,400 need any medical assistance as a result of going to the park. That's a tiny fraction of 1 per cent of visitors. Most of these have minor bumps caused by not following safety rules. It is not the extreme rides that cause the most injuries. One of the most common injuries is a bump on the head after falling from a horse on the carousel!

Safe design and operation

All rides are designed and constructed with safety in mind. Brakes exert more friction than is actually needed to stop a moving rollercoaster car. Hills and curves are sized and shaped so they do not create unsafe amounts of centripetal and G-forces. Computer systems are used to control the speed of cars, the distance between them and any obstructions on tracks.

HIGH-G EFFECTS

The fastest amusement park rides, such as loop-the-loops, take riders up to about 3 or 4 G. Pilots blasting upwards in space rockets or fighter jets turning at high speed may experience up to 12 G. At this acceleration, their blood would flow towards their feet due to inertia, which might cause them to faint because their brain does not have enough blood. So pilots wear special suits that press on their blood vessels to stop the blood moving to the wrong places.

Did you feel the force?

Most people's memories of a day at the amusement park include the bright lights and colours, the looks on excited, happy and scared faces, and the sounds of joy and terror. But the real stars of the show are silent, invisible, powerful forces that make the rides such an assault on our senses.

Stars of the show

The main acts are gravity, acceleration, friction and centripetal forces. But they rely on a supporting cast. These include other invisible assistants, such as inertia, and potential and kinetic energy. They also include the rides themselves, from the shapes of the curves and loops to the devices that send rollercoasters to the top of their first hill and those that stop machines from speeding out of control. The whole production is the work of park designers, safety experts and, of course, the riders themselves!

Freefall Xtreme and other wind tunnel rides are massive, upwards-pointing fans. Riders can float on the spot, cheating gravity.

Old and new

Some park rides have been with us for years, such as the helter-skelter, carousel and rotor. But designers have had to build bigger, faster and more exciting rides over time to keep the crowds visiting amusement parks. In the mid-1960s, the highest rollercoaster was 33 metres (100 feet), but today some tower nearly five times that height and reach speeds of 240 kilometres (150 miles) per hour.

Today, many people are used to playing exciting video games with virtual thrills and spills in their homes, so amusement park designers are constantly developing new rides to attract the crowds. For example, the riders on Harry Potter and the Forbidden Journey sit on benches moved around by robotic arms mounted on tracks, which move past 3D screens and through spaces based on the Harry Potter film sets. It is a cross between a simulator and a real ride with some real forces. Just imagine what rides will be like in future!

Quiz

1 The initial potential energy of a rollercoaster is changed into what after it crests the first hill?
- a) more potential energy
- b) electrical energy
- c) light energy
- d) kinetic energy

2 What are the two main forces acting on a rollercoaster car going downhill?
- a) gravity and acceleration
- b) gravity and friction
- c) acceleration and deceleration
- d) friction and acceleration

3 Newton's first law of motion says that an object in motion tends to what?
- a) pick up friction
- b) stay in motion
- c) eventually stop moving
- d) accelerate

4 When an object falls, air resistance:
- a) acts in the opposite direction to the weight
- b) acts in the same direction as the weight
- c) acts at right angles to the weight
- d) does not act at all

5 If gravity pulls you towards the centre of Earth, why don't you fall through the floor?
- a) because gravity runs out
- b) because gravity doesn't act through hard floors
- c) because the floor exerts an equal force to gravity in the opposite direction
- d) because of friction

6 What is the force pulling an object moving in a circle that prevents it flying off in a straight line?
a) centrifugal force
b) inertia
c) centripetal force
d) friction

7 Which two of the following are not forces?
a) mass
b) gravity
c) height
d) thrust

8 When an object is at rest or stationary:
a) there are no forces acting on it
b) there are forces acting on it, but they are balanced
c) there is just one force, gravity, acting on it
d) there are forces acting on it, but they are unbalanced

9 Which of the following is a change of motion?
a) speed
b) inertia
c) acceleration
d) friction

10 When you are falling on a drop tower and experiencing weightlessness, the G-force you feel is:
a) exactly 1-G
b) 2-G
c) 10-G
d) zero-G

Answers
1 d; 2 b; 3 b; 4 a; 5 d; 6 c; 7 a and c; 8 b; 9 c; 10 d

Glossary

accelerate   move more quickly, speed up

air resistance   force that slows down the movement of an object through the air

balanced   when two forces acting on an object are equal in size but act in opposite directions, we say that they are balanced forces

centripetal force   force that makes an object follow a curved path that is pointed towards the centre point the object moves around. Spin a toy on a string and the centripetal force is towards your hand.

cockpit   compartment where pilot and other crew of an aircraft sit and work

deceleration   slowing down or negative acceleration

electrical circuit   unbroken path along which electrical energy or electricity flows to make electrical devices work

force   a push or a pull on an object. A force gives energy to an object.

friction   force produced when one surface moves over another surface. Friction acts to slow down the movement.

G-force   measure of how much force acts on a person or an object compared with the normal weight force due to Earth's gravity

gravity   force of attraction between two objects. On Earth, gravity pulls everything towards the ground. This is because Earth's mass is much greater than everything around it.

hydraulic jack   machine that uses trapped liquid in tubes to create pushes and pulls

inertia   resistance to change in direction or speed. Inertia is greater in objects with greater mass.

inner ear   part of the ear inside our head. It detects sounds and gravity, which helps us to keep our balance.

inversion   stretches of rollercoaster rides when people are suspended upside down

kinetic energy   energy a moving object has because it is moving

mass   amount of matter or physical substance something has. Weight is related to mass because weight measures the force of gravity on the mass of an object.

non-contact force   force that acts on an object without touching it, such as magnetism or gravity

potential energy   ability to do work caused by an object's position, tension, electric charge or other factors. For example, a squashed spring and a book high on a shelf both have potential energy.

receptors   special cells in living things that can detect changes in light, pressure and other stimuli

revolution   complete turn or spin about a fixed point. Spinning speed is often expressed in revolutions per minute, or rpm.

simulator   machine in some amusement parks that mimics a real ride using film and the movements of people's seats

terminal velocity   constant speed that a falling object reaches when air resistance balances gravity

unbalanced   when one force acting on an object is greater in size than the other force, we say that they are unbalanced forces

vertical   upright or at right angles to the horizontal

weightlessness   floating feeling people get when there is no force of support on their body

zero G   when there is no apparent force of gravity acting on a body

Books

Forces and Motion (Essential Physical Science), Angela Royston (Raintree, 2014)

Forces and Motion (Science Detective Investigates), Katie Dicker (Wayland, 2011)

Gut-wrenching Gravity and Other Fatal Forces (Disgusting and Dreadful Science), Anna Claybourne (Franklin Watts, 2013)

Rollercoasters (Go Turbo), Jim Brush (Franklin Watts, 2011)

Websites

www.areavibes.com/library/roller-coaster-history
This is a fascinating website that gives you information about how rollercoasters have changed through history.

www-g.eng.cam.ac.uk/mmg/teaching/peterstidwill/interact/ resources/parkworldplot/parkworldplotlink.htm
Click on "launch the game" and explore a virtual amusement park, encountering forces as you go. You will find lots of clear information and discover a range of rides.

www.learner.org/interactives/parkphysics/coaster
Surely you're itching to design your own rollercoaster after reading this book! If so, visit this site and test how hill height, shape, loop height and other features will affect your ride.

www.pbslearningmedia.org/asset/mck05_int_rollercoaster
See the changing kinetic and potential energy amounts as a rollercoaster moves through a complete ride.

Places to visit

Science Museum
Exhibition Road
South Kensington
London SW7 2DD

www.sciencemuseum.org.uk

This is the world's largest science museum of its kind. It has 40 galleries that explore scientific breakthroughs and include hands-on exhibits.

There are thousands of amusement parks worldwide, including these thrilling ones in the UK:

* Alton Towers, Staffordshire   **www.altontowers.com**
* Legoland Windsor, Windsor   **www.legoland.co.uk**
* Thorpe Park, Chertsey, Surrey   **www.thorpepark.com**

Further research

* Research amusement parks worldwide and then create a global map of attractions. Where are the highest and fastest rides or the tallest drop towers? From your research, do you think that amusement parks are distributed evenly around the globe or only in particular continents or countries? Do they tally with the population and average income (GDP) of each country? Why do you think this is?

* Build your own rollercoaster using curtain rail or foam pipe insulation tube for a track and marbles for cars (see www.msichicago.org/online-science/activities/activity-detail/activities/build-a-roller-coaster/browseactivities/0). Experiment with different shaped loop-the-loops, twists and other features. Can you make your marble experience an inversion?

* Amusement parks are at particular fixed places, but many people can experience rides at travelling fairs. Research the history of fairs. Have they always been just for amusement?